A STRING OF PEARLS

To: Eleanor

Best Wishes Always.

Love Pat.

A STRING
OF
PEARLS

Poems about People and Places and Life

JACQUE DALEY

JACPAK BOOKS
Florida

For Information Address:

Jacpak Books
17650 N.W 22nd Avenue
Miami, Florida 33056

Printed in the United States of America

Library of Congress
Catalog Card Number 98-92136

ISBN 0-9667429-0-7

To All Those who Treasure Life.

CONTENTS

Foreword
Acknowledgments

Foreword

To write about people, places and life means to
delve into creation, exposing the mysteries of life.
A String of Pearls is filled with blistering sincerity,
and provocating thoughts and ideas. The variety in
her poems I find very refreshing. She began by
encouraging the weak, *Joy Comes in the Morning*
and exalting the strong, *The Patron Saint of
Bellerose.*

With her penetrating eye, Jacque has seen right
through the human heart capturing occasions of love
and laughter, its hidden desires and sometimes
thwarted aspirations. As in life so in memories, the
sweet is laced with the bitter, at times agonizing, at
times triumphant.

The poems speak to us from the pages,
stirring recollections from the past and helping us to
see ourselves at times jokingly, anew.

A sincere appreciation of God and his creation is
profoundly manifested in verses creatively written
that readers will find spiritually and morally
uplifting.

A String of Pearls is a beautifully written collection
of poems that will stand the test of time.

Deepak Sawlani MD

Acknowledgments

Special thanks to the Currans for the way they have touched my life and my work. Mrs. C, without you I wouldn't have accomplished this much. To Nina, thanks for everything, you are truly a wonderful person.

To Doug, I'm eternally grateful.

To John and Carol, you have the greatest gift in life (knowing how to enjoy it), thank you for your support and admiration of my talents.

To Mary, Claude, Beth, T.T, C.J, you are all so full of life, keep the spirit.

Elaine, Chris, Melissa, Trevor, thanks for your help and occasional chit-chat, a million thanks for your help Charlie.

Kathy, Ann, Janet, Jimmy and families your thoughtfulness have not gone unnoticed. To Kevin, hang in there, we'll meet one day.

To Police Officer Beggins and his two daughters Emily and Hannah, you have made many of my 'gray days sunny'.

To Amy and Maggie, smile and the sun comes out.

To Jeanne and Jerry, Ed and Rosie, Mrs. Quinn.

To Mr. and Mrs. Macari Sr., Patrice, Tracy, Kate and their families .

To members of my family who have made positive contributions to my life and work.

I'll take time out to say a big THANKS to you all and may your lives be richly blessed.

Joy Comes in The Morning

It is with such jubilance-
that I think of him,
the one who fashioned
my heart-
in perfect rhythm.

With sheer enchantment
I walk-
through Pastures Green,
with roses, daises, daffodils-
his omnipresence unseen.

Who wouldn't the darkness fear-
with ghostly shadows around,
where evil crawls
unsuspectingly-
apprehension abounds.

But in him is my delight-
my hope and ecstasy,
and when fear disappears
with night-
my courage returns to me.

1

The Patron Saint of Bellerose

"You didn't know him?"
She asked ,
shaking her head,
"a wonderful man, very kind,
they don't come any better."

I wondered in amazement.
Five years since he passed,
but they never cease to speak of him,
with such passion.
"I imagine I missed knowing
a great person,"
I said with sincerity.

And at the photograph on the mantle,
I often stop to stare,
drawn by the magic of twinkling eyes,
sharp with wit and wisdom profound.
And SHE also spoke of him,
endearingly,
of his patience and gentleness,
his great knowledge and insight.

Oft times, my hand I'd run
along his dust-covered leather bound books,
possibly in the hope of finding some treasure.
And always there would be
some intriguing mystery,
knowledge yet to be discovered.

And I believe every word they said,
when they spoke

with such fondness,
of the way he would always
scrape the top
of the ice-cream bucket
'to make it even'.

And then I wished
he hadn't gone so soon.
But still I reasoned,
it was his spirit that led me
to the one in need,
and his presence still
pervades the house where
he watches over his loved ones.

*Title courtesy of J. Curran Jr.

3

Musings of The Heart

One fine day
upon a rock I sat
and myself began to muse
but in short time
I became perplexed.
So I beckon to
the powers that be,
to kindly court me
with some poetry.

I thought Thalia,
my is empty,
to me talk some comedy
and bucolic.
And Calliope,
my eloquence is
quite lacking,
with no verse heroic
to give luster.

So flat my lyrics are,
Erato,
with nothing of love
to give flair.
Yet but a minute,
I was graced in a flash
and I began
to write poetry
with quite a dash.

Midnight

The moon may hide
its face if so inclines,
crickets chirping, the cat
calls its mate
across the fence

Lovers hands entwined
under starry skies.
The widow
dreams
of life that was,
the maiden
of life that will be.

Nothing moves,
everything quiet.
Until bursting with life
twilight gives way
to morning bright.

Mount Olympus

O throne of Zeus
now you stand
empty,
'neath puffs of clouds.

Is the power
of Zeus no more
able to direct
the mortal soul.

Is your voice
no longer heard on high
like thunder in the sky.
Nor your shrieks echoed
as lightening strikes.

O Zeus,
what made you vacate
your throne
which now stands
a heap of stone?

Hieroglyphics

Ourselves,
much like books we write
daily on each page.
Words uttered,
deeds done,
enough to compile
a volume or two.
Prints in black or white,
embossed, italics
and bold colored-images
make things bright.

At times the print
is hard to read,
as the pun and satire
seek to deceive.
And then the book
is much like a film,
each scene an act
and not from within.
Oft times the story
is one long theme,
in others each chapter
presents a different scene.

Fiction and non-fiction
side by side on the shelf,
readers baffled,
as ambiguity jump
from pages
too worn
to be legible.

The Hands of Time

You sit-
on my nightstand,
the mantle-
wherever you can be-
conspicuously.
Tick. Tick.

How you dabble in our lives-
before we were born-
our mother's labor
contractions-
you spaced them at will.
Tick. Tick.

You set the time for school and play-
for dinner and for bed.
And when grown-
with responsibilities-
the time for me to wed.
Tick. Tick.

You set the alarm of
our biological clock-
which ticks not only in our head,
when on our bed sick we lay-
you're hurrying us on to be dead.
Tick. Tick.

The Beggar

"Ma'am," he said,
"a quarter have you got."
Not a morsel for a meal
or a place to lay his head,
unkempt,
in a corner of the street,
the beggar sat
Day in, day out.

And the passersby
who didn't stop
he would curse out,
"This isn't what I always was,
this isn't always me,
this isn't what I used to be
before better times turn bad."

He'd sit and shout,
lifting his voice
in bitterness,
lifting his voice
in misery.
Day in, day out.

And should we go home
and our trappings
take off
even for a day.
How close would be
the resemblance
when next to the beggar
we stand.

A Courtesy Title

Awashed in tears,
sackcloth on your head,
mourning your lover.
Bidding goodbye,
your godhead sways
from too much wine.
Would Nelson and Churchill rise
now defending a spoilt prize?

The brightest gems fallen
from your crown
and those remaining
struggling with dust.
Does Victoria turns in her grave
when monarchy runs awry?
When discord spits in the eye
of sovereignty.

Ah, but who could resist
the scandal,
and what if the guillotine
could talk still?
Whose head would it choose
in order to keep honor?

A Beautiful Woman

to Mimi

Wish I were as she,
whom Venus and
Aphrodite has outrun,
yet still a gift
molded for the gods.

It ran deep her beauty,
as outward grace
melts with inner style.
The sweetness
of inspiration
coats her words
as her voice
carries on the wind
like windchimes.

And nothing could
emaciate a frown,
instead, a smile
overshadows
all misdeeds.

The Separation

'Twas but for a brief moment,
but seemed like eternity.
The separation,
brought days of loneliness
and nights of emptiness.

Like a chasm,
the longing to see
your soft reassuring smile,
unbearable.
From differing ends,
'twas the magic
that brought us close.

And suddenly,
the realization,
affections deep
and boundless as the sea,
its wave caressing
every mood
and cresting toward
a restful shore.

And
the sensations,
never ebbing,
but flowing
always
to different grounds.

An Episode

So profound,
so intense,
the anxiety
ignites flames
within my breast,
searing my brain,
the memory
of the last kiss,
the dread
of the next meeting.

Is love so
confounded
then to detest,
now to desire,
can a love
seemingly cold
burn so hot.

Morning Ride

A breath of fresh air
and the city scurries,
neatly dressed,
crisply neat and rapid
footsteps tread
the pathways.
The train moves
smoothly, quickly,
with its perfumed load,
neatly packed.

Crisp,
the morning news
engrossed a reader,
so too the book
with the marker.
Thirty-fourth street
then forty-second.

In short time
each rushes
to meet his
days burden.
And I'm left
neatly wondering
what my next move
should be.

Evening Ride

Shoveling,
bumping,
butts-a-thumping,
the rush hour crowd
squeezed.

Crumpled
news,
no longer fresh,
bunched
under sweaty arms.

And
the unfinished book
struggled
with weary eyes
as anxious hearts
anticipate stops
that now seem
twice as long.

Then the tired train
stops
and spews
its heavy load.

The Lonely Church

Sharp features
etched against the skyline,
the steeple stood -
a weary travelers lighthouse.
Sundays are
well-wishers packed
to overflowing.
Welcomed, are those who
for a refreshing come.

But oft times in solitude,
the church stood
on a lonely hill.
The ghosts
of its graveyard
play music
without an audience.

So I can think of another,
lifting spirits
and bringing good cheer.
Yet time after time
alone
on his lonely hill stood,
haunted by the ghosts
of his memories,
playing on the keys
of his mind.

A Helping Hand

I woke up this morning
and wondered
"what could I do to make
this world a better place?"

My heart sank when I saw
how much was needed
to further uplift
the human race.

Before long the first task
came my way, I smiled
and felt great joy when
with another he repaid.

As I walked along the pathway
I saw another burdened with care,
it took but just a moment
to help erased his fears.

My task seemed so much lighter
than when I had at first begun,
two more sad souls
I helped to cheer
before the set of sun.

When at last I was forced to retire
from a duty which I could not tire,
my heart swelled and
my spirit lifted, knowing
tomorrow is another day to give.

The Broken Mirror

Peering through
the windows of my soul
the gray mist rises,
settling on painful thoughts.

In the distance,
a door slammed shut
as I struggled
against the rope
yoked around my neck.

Yanked
from an intended path
I stumbled.
The bittersweet joys
and pale sorrows
in the same cup
brimming with hope.

Tribal Dance

They asked me my name.
I am still not sure.
It has changed over the years.
Only an
X
marked the place
where I was born.

At times
I hear low thumping sounds,
the sounds of drums.
I try to comprehend,
but it is too faint,
too distant.
Lost between generations,
four or five or six.

The ship
did not return to take us back,
we waited in vain
still groping in the dark.

Who is First

I'm on this side   you are on that,
we decide to step   over the boundaries
          and meet on the line.

We had a union,
then two
and three,
a new generation
with no clear identity
will keep running
until the color fades.

Only a man
or a woman
since we all are one
in the race.

Ode to Life

Throw off now your cloak
of darkness,
enticed by a tranquilized brain.
For Hades provides only
a euphoric bed
that collapses under the
weight of morning.

Be parasites to edifices
bequeathed by ancestors
in the tradition of the
Archimedes'
and Galileos
and glean the legacies
of the da Vincis
and Picassos,
the Mozarts
and the Bachs.

A pilgrimage
is your journey,
its course the essence
of unbridled dreams
ushered on by the tide
of aspirations.

Ode to Youth

Awake!
Your day is dawning,
your breasts as Mont Blanc
now stand, the gems of
your diadem yet undiscovered.

With the swiftness of the
Gazelle and the surety
of the Mountain Goat,
the globe is the maze to
your destination.

Arise!
And in the Summer of your days,
feast your eyes on
soulful food. And entreat
the ear to find solace in
sounds melodious.

For when winter locks
the doors, the rooms are
in a coffin laid and
the strength of the hand
unable to lift the lid.

Ode to Freedom

How high does the
unfettered spirit soars,
amidst time.
In wild abandonment
his creativity
unsurpassed.

In the prison of the soul
is no judge appellate
to unshackle
perceptions of biased
thoughts
that blocks
the stymied mind.

Ode to peace

The turmoil mind wears
a mantle of opposition and
becomes an Anaconda
slithering in hostility.

An ever hungry vulture
on the threshold of time,
that feeds its babes through
tubes - a brackish victual.

Wrest the keys from
the Halcyon and open
the doors to the calm seas,
or else seek him
in the rivulets of the mind.

Would they that knew
the idyllic mind
find the path
to Nirvana
the paradise
of the soul.

Ode to Courage

In martyrdom
and gallantry
he finds his
sweetest repose,
and in his medium
the undaunted soul
has no boundaries.

His hands open wide
the dark curtains
that drape
our dubious minds
and lay bare
the less travelled road,
whisking
our fears behind.

His worth lies
not only in the Epee,
but so too in simple
acts of courtesy,
in telling truths
unashamedly and
supporting your beliefs
wholeheartedly.

Ode to Justice

You who hold the balance
upon your shoulders
with unbiased strength,
shout to deafened ears
with your impartial tongue.

Strike back, when
judges would tip the
contents of the scale
under their gowns
and hide indifference
in their jowls.

And the silence of your
pounding gavel
will hammer throughout
the shuttered courtrooms,
as your long arm
spans the reaches
of adversity.

Ode to Love

Time was-
you were-
brailled
and my fingers read you-
knowingly.

How my heart
did sing- then-
the most melodious birds-
captivating-
with sweet tunes.

Now
through spectacled eyes-
your bearded smile
I see-
the more wise.

And now
my heart sings-
songs unchanged-
to a tune
more mellow.

Feet that Talk

A man
upholding the law,
they said
he'd gone
and done them wrong.
But was it a fault
of he to them
or one of he to her?

So he tried
to fix his wrong,
expressing remorse
and rue.
But when a heart
has gone astray
can it still be true?

Master of the Game

I stepped down,
down, down, down,
down into the deep dark of the hold
where bodies melt with darkness,
leaving only the white of the eye,
the sound of chains
and groans of pain
and moans of woe.

I stepped up,
up, up, up,
up on to the auction block,
where nice gentlemen
in Fedoras and breeches
looked at my head, into my nose
and all the way down to my toes,
then placed their bids.

I stepped out,
out, out, out,
out into the bright sunshine,
where the canefields
stood in theWest Indies
and the cotton fields
of the Deep South
(in North America I mean).

I stepped in,
in, in, in,
into the shade,
not to cool my head
but to tread (the wheel that is).
And to feel the cat

(the one with nine tails I mean)
claw its way into my back.

The pain I felt,
the scream I stifled
even with the little one still inside.
I paused for a moment,
to give birth
to a new generation,
carrying a torch not yet lit.

I stepped on,
on, on, on,
on to the plank of the gallows
for today I shall die.
Frustrated
I tried to run away,
now they are making
an example of me.

Two hundred years since
but I still am,
through reincarnation
I strive to exist.

And now,
I step down,
down, down, down,
down into the plushness
of my carpeted penthouse,
from where I survey the world
and make strategic decisions.

Then I step up,
up, up, up,
up the steps of my private jet,
which shall take me to Rio, Africa
and South America.

I step out,
out, out, out,
out into the bright sunshine
of the West Indies and Africa and
The Far East.
I survey my investments
in land and factories and buildings.

I step in,
in, in, in,
into the coolness of my Jacuzzi,
to cool my head after a long day.
I pause to give birth,
to a new generation
carrying a torch,
lit with hopes and dreams.

And I sail on,
on, on, on,
on the ship of ambition,
of fame and of fortune.
And in the light
I can see every form
and stare into the white of every eye,
for now

I have become

MASTER OF THE GAME.

On High

Dispersed, they stood,
sentries clad in white.
At other times,
obediently they go,
where e'er the wind
will blow.

A constant reminder
of a roof over our heads,
though boundless
the sky may seem.

Puffed, now they are,
dark and ever brooding,
heralding the onset
of rain and showers
quite soothing.

A constant reminder
of God's continuous
blessings, though far
away he may seem.

Mutations

Confounded is
the level of humanity
that hides behind
the armor of reverence.
While the swords
of bigotry and injustice
steal the lives of babes
sleeping in the night.

With senses of imbalance
and insecurity,
manifested in
predators likeness,
swelling the hunters snare.
Possessing the odor
of a conqueror's weakness
entrenched in a victor's smile.

And behind closed doors
they talk of peace,
of ending holy wars.
And the irony,
finally complete,
the begetting of peace
through war.

Fear

It grips you
like the pangs of hunger,
stomach churning,
it cuts like a knife.
It's eyes as of the tiger
in the night sees
what is not there.
And your crippled feet
go running,
from what
you do not know.

The adrenaline
keeps pumping.
Sweaty palms grasp
what they cannot hold.
The panic attacks your
scared throat,
tying knots,
and you dread
the anxious thoughts.
And you cannot wake up
until your eyelid
screams.

The Mountain Builders

They came,
carried on the crest of waves
and borne by highfloating clouds.
Through conquering and claiming
and afterwards visiting and pleading ,
they came.

And in their hand,
a new dream of tomorrow,
of streets paved with gold.
Yet by the stark realization
they were not deterred,
but laid the foundation,
brick by brick.

The Pizzerias and Restaurants, the
Laundromats and Cleaners.
And what of the Firefighters, Policemen
and teachers too.
And weren't marble tiles scrubbed shine
and laundry kept fresh
until the mistresses came home.

And what about their babes,
even from a few months
entrusted in the care of nannies,
until they should be on their way
to be the leaders of tomorrow.

Such a great nation
in the palms of a few hands.
And this so families in another land

could eat bread
and have a dream too.

Of the atrocities of the holocaust
we were reminded,
of the tragedy of the Titanic too.
From the East, North,
South and West,
the four corners of the world.
And the flow never stopped,
the Mountain Builders.
They came.

And neither did they put down all
that they carried with them.
For in every Chinatown
there is a Pagoda,
in every Little India the Taj Mahal.
On many corners the
Mosque and Synagogue
stand erect.

The African drum still beats loudly
as the aroma from Caribbean pots
float on the air.
And the flow never stopped,
the Mountain Builders,
They came.

An Aphrodisiac

Once upon a time
our love was
on a platter
bound for the Heavens.

You Adonis,
I Aphrodite
on feathered bed
ensconced.

Our insatiable appetites
grazed
with the music
of our souls.

The Temptress

Even as a babe,
she embraced me warmly.
And with spoonfuls,
keeping in check
her full strength.

And as a young man,
taking me under her wings,
like a fortress in stormy weather,
protecting me
from the elements.

And,
knowledge,
twisting her arms around my neck
as an ardent lover
welcomes a new love.
spurring me in directions
hitherto unforeseen.
And often times cradling my head
in the crevasses of rocks, to rest.

And in the night a beautiful spirit,
standing over me
and smiling seductively.
And I,arising instantly,
as she beckoned for me to follow.
Even as the mist descended heavily,
I struggled to keep up with her,
unable to discern
the path before me,
at times stumbling

39

over rocks and debris
but never giving up the pursuit.

But picking up speed,
she bounded,
over hills and plains,
wisdom,
a gazelle no doubt,
smooth and graceful.

And of the faithful along the way
I inquired,
the crevasses in their faces
comparing with time.
They would answer,
always something different,
always something new.

And to my chest
I clutched these treasures,
ever so tightly,
knowing I'd need them
along the way,
as I pursued,
my journey endless.

A glance sideways,
and fortune distracts.
A sly one, as a ghost in the night,
now here, then disappearing.
A strange one she is,
at times rewarding the reckless
without pitying the deserving,
and smiling only with a few.

But constantly luring,
scattering trinkets along the way,
though nothing compares
to her golden slippers
making music on the rocky path.
At times they would
all meet in one place,
heralding the birth of a mortal soul
and giving divers blessings,
but the occasions rare.

And,
do I willingly surrender to them,
these mistresses of our fate?
Always in sight
but never giving wholly
of themselves,
gambling over our souls,
even as time trashes our body
senseless.

Morphing

Walking one summer's day,
a host of butterflies
I did see,
amazed at their colors
and designs
I ponder their creation
and find
that the beautiful butterflies
from caterpillars
did climb.

This made me think about
humanity,
and a similar pattern
I did see,
how our own lives
could be cocoons
and by our own magic
at any stage
ourselves into
beautiful butterflies
we could change.

The World's a Stage

It's all an act,
this thing called life,
that we should perform
to prevent strife.

So when you are rich,
then be poor
lest the gods of poverty
should come knocking at your door.

And when you are happy,
do not make your countenance so,
for the fates observing,
your good fortune may desire.

For misery loves company,
it's said and it's true
and the one in ire
should want it transported to you.

Grasp age when young,
for the aged do have much
by knowledge and experience.
And when old relive youth
then you shall enjoy
the best of both worlds.

But if you wish to sit astride the world
and pacify it too,
do not wage war
if peace is eschewed.

43

For a soul set on fire
will have no calm
and by any means necessary,
does not put it on par.

O Fair Isle

O beautiful Isle, I long to see,
to feel your fresh breath
upon my face.
Your sparkling blue waters
will soothe my parched skin,
and my head the swaying palms
will cradle in the shade.

None can compare
to your beauty so fair,
a gem of the Indies you are.
For many have come
to taste of your love
and always keep coming
back for more.

The Flora, the Fauna, the People,
are some of the many dishes
you have to offer.
Your hills and mountains
steep, contrast
with your sea and valleys deep.

I wait,
with breath abated,
until your beauty
I once more behold,
to satisfy this deep longing
in my soul.

Borrowed Times

We are leased from him
our days,
numbered,
as night runs into day.
The hours are
for us to use,
to labor for him
and pray.

We shall account
for each day spent
in toil or liberty.
How sweet the rewards
for those who will
a place in paradise be.

Uppercrust

Baking
in the sun all day
then in
Jacuzzi to cool.
Alimony of
celebrity
and wall street
boom
grease limousine
wheels.

Does not take much
by way of brain
to see
through
this facade,
desperate souls
in need
of repair.

The Malady

A tiny lump
growing in the head
and like a wild vine
did spread.
And it grew.

Nothing was done
for it to contain,
it metastasizes
to the toe.
It grew.

In a bed,
sick she lay
with no repent
or to pray.
It grew.

A little while
and she was dead,
her eulogy they read,
"it's so sad
she could not see
what a killer
jealousy can be."

Of Selfish Possession

A beautiful dove
that cooed so sweet
I thought I should
possess the bird.

I very soon clipped its wings
and to keep in tow,
on its foot put a string.
It could not fly and did not sing
and very soon it was dead.

A blackbird then I saw,
that shrieked and
shrilled and screamed.
I sought to let it loose
so far from me it would go.

Toward the sky it soared,
a beautiful thing
that meets the eye.
Its shrieking became a melody,
a pleasant thing to the ear.

It very soon
came back to me
and has been since
my best of friend.

Angel in Disguise

It's not the curl
of the hair,
nor the pout
of the lips.
Not the busty
chest,
nor the swinging
hips.
Its the magic.

Not the criss-
crossing legs,
nor the extended
derriere,
that I have not.

Its the voice
that sings
with the wind
tunes to cheer
your heart.
The way I cradled
your head
when you
were wounded.
That's the magic.

The Unending Wall

We chipped away
brick by brick,
even from the age of three.
Chipping away,
climbing,
in an effort to be free.

Through Nursery,
thro' Kindergarten,
even Elementary.
Up the ladder,
through attaining a first degree,
many chipped,
through the masters to the Ph.D..

And when done
taking a survey,
what did we see,
the wall broken only
by a fraction,
minutely.
So we stopped
not willing to take
anymore test.

Then a look sideways,
just by a glance
we see,
we could just as easily
climb over
the fence.

But How Marcus Garvey

Was the
Black Starliner
nothing but a dream,
sailing down the Nile
of your
imagination.

Or was it suppose
to be
the reverse
of what had
gone on before.
A transport for
colored bodies
across
the ocean floor.

In Arlington Cemetery

The tombstones
lovingly mark the place
where the nations best
are laid to rest,
who had great courage
to do their part
in whatever deed
was for them ordained.

Like the wind
rolling over hills and plains,
they gave of themselves
and held nothing back.
And as flowers in bloom
they grew in God's grace.
So now for them
we secure this place
of quiet rest and solitude.

To The Musicians

O hurry now
and come to us,
quench our thirsty souls
with your beating drums
and strumming guitars.
And with wings furnish us -
as we soar towards
immortality.

Feed us
the cord that will inspire us ,
to live, to love,
to rise above the dust -
of human misery.
Make our senses dull
with your
sweet crooning.

As the melodies
trace pathways
through our veins,
our voices strain
to echo your blues,
even as our hearts
do swell to bursting-
with your rhythm.

And
when you have embalmed us
with heavenly chords,
shroud us
in rhapsodies so divine,

54

illuminating the
common thread
that binds us.

Meditation

I sense the power
of God within me.
When God is within me,
I feel a profound
sense of freedom.
Freedom
from the shackles of misery
and the burden of guilt,
Freedom from hate
and malice.

Freedom to love,
to care, to give, to share.
Freedom
that comes from having faith.
And with that faith
comes security
and self-confidence,
knowing he dwells within me.

When God dwells
within me,
I feel his presence
everywhere.
I see him
in the things he created,
in the flowers
and in the animals,
and in the precious life
he gives to us.

I hear his voice

in the soft rustle of the wind,
in the sweet melody
of the singing birds.
Then I know
he not only dwells within me
but surrounds me.

When God surrounds me,
his powerful spirit
protects me.
He gives me
the whole armor
that fortifies me
against evil,
and guides me
in the right path.

In Appreciation

How majestic are the mountains
wherein lies his strength,
the soft clouds floating
transports his gentle spirit.

The lightening and thunder,
enough to cause a trance,
then we see how small the world is
even at a glance.

Musing at the beauty
of the flower in the garden,
and with remorse as sinners
we seek his pardon.

Would our hearts respond
to his loving touch,
even in everything
he has given so much.

The beauty that surrounds us
we often take for granted,
if we would only take time to see
his love in them imparted.

Lord,
grant us a little understanding,
to appreciate in thy creation
the glory of thy blessing.

Awesome Awareness

His radiance envelopes
my simple form,
winds caressing,
feeling soft as silk
He's the freshness
of the air I breathe
and the tremor of the earth
quaking beneath my feet.

Like the blood
coursing through my veins,
like the particles
in the tiny drops of rain,
His presence pervades,
in the fragrance
of the roses wet with dew,
and the flowers with such
wonderful hue.

He's the universe,
the sun, the moon,
star and earth.
He's the hope
of our second birth.
He's unchanging
firm as ever.
He's Today, Tomorrow
and Forever.

This Day is Ours

Let's live for Today.
And while we live Today
enjoy all the good things
that Today has brought
while we wait
for Tomorrow.

And if and when
Tomorrow comes,
we'll live for all
it has brought Today,
the good and the bad,
the happy and the sad.

And when Tomorrow
comes Today,
Today becomes
Yesterday
and is buried
in antiquity.

Like Gibraltar

to Eileen

Though the years
paint wrinkles on her face
she stood, in defiance,
courting immortality.

Her hands
span three generations, yet
she can still walk
in the last one's shoes.

Though her memory
ticks like a clock
painfully out of sync,
her duties
she can still recall,
at the kitchen sink.

Seventy years
she stood,
staring in space,
for the coming of our Lord
and at humanity's
disgrace.

A tower of strength
she is, strengthening
her children.
She stands, strong
and tall,
like a rock.

The Straight Way

A labyrinth
this life is,
with intricacies
abound
to put one
in a daze.

The many paths
crisscrossing,
simply a mass
of confusion
has us in
disarray.

Amazed

Is this my life
I see before me?
A maze of
streets and avenues,
highways and byways.

Trials and temptations
dotting every corner,
fame and fortune
lining the way.

Sometimes dark,
sometimes bright,
I have to be careful
lest I stray.

Stop signs and
speed limits
in appropriate places,
I dare not disobey.

And if I should
complete my journey,
I'd notice in it a cycle.
It ended
where it had begun,
twice a child,
once a man.

Of Man And Nature

He roared
and his voice echoed in thunder,
without warning he struck,
her emotions torn asunder,
as a streak of lightening
strikes the tree in its pathway.
A force to be reckoned with
is nature,
so is a man with a malady.

And,
tears stained her cheeks
like the rain
on the window pane as it streaks.
Her figure slumped
and she began to shake,
as the earth tremors
during a quake.
Her face, snow white with fear,
begging for mercy.

Then,
like the ebbing sea
with sudden remorse,
he embraced her with such calm,
as of the eye during a storm.
Softly, he kissed her forehead.
She looked up and smiled,
and as she does it lit her face
as the rainbow lights the sky
after the rain.

He held her close,
she knew he loved her,
but it brought such pain,
like the rage of the elements
that disturb
the summer's day.

From whence they came
she could not say,
neither could she understand
his uncontrollable rage.
And why not make love
and not war,
as in the old adage.

Mesmerized

Swinging hips
in the pale evening light,
heels clicking
down the dusty pavement.

Air intoxicating
and the magic of the night,
nothing felt wrong,
everything felt right.

A seductive smile,
the flutter of lids
were all that were needed
to place his bid.

He did not notice
until it was too late
that he had committed sin
and deceived his mate.

The thought and memories
now smart,
how could he threw away
what he had for nought.

So the rest of his days
he spent in the pub drinking ale
and telling all
of the wife
and child he'd fail.

The Flirt

Beware the Flirt,
as his eyelids flutter,
he'll steal your heart
as he engages
in light chatter.
His smiles are nothing
but wiles,
just a part of his
many styles.

Beware the Flirt,
ladies hold on to
your skirts,
he'll pretend
to be rich,
but owns only
on his back the shirt.
He'll speak of things
that he has not seen,
but this is just a part
of his scheme.

Beware the Flirt,
he'll try to get
your attention,
but of his true self
he will not mention.
He will say things
to evince laughter,
but only until
he gets
what he's after.

The Elusive

Dreaming
of a childhood sweetheart
brought back
memories intoxicatingly sweet.

A first kiss
in the house of horrors,
an omen?

For love
has now become like ghosts
to haunt and jeer.

The eerie midnight feelings,
disappearing
at the break of dawn.

An Obsession

I searched for you,
over the river banks
where the water rose high,
in the pasture green
where daffodils play,
on the hilltops
where mountain goats roam,
In the valley deep
where fairies are fast asleep.

I searched for you,
in the treetop
where the crow makes its nest,
in the caves
where bats do dwell,
where cows
are milking in the barn.
I was tired and came home
to find you
waiting there for me.

The Stranger

A stranger walked into my life-
adventuring
and suddenly everything bright
and changing.
In corners once dank and drear,
the sun was now shining.

The rainbow had the clouds
in contest,
the flowers began to look
their best,
The chirping of the birds took wings
and as melodiously flew.

A smile I saw on every face
lighting,
as I bid them a bright hello.
Life never felt
so exciting
until the day I met the stranger.

Midnight Musings

His face looms large
from the ceiling
and my heart quivers
with excitement.
The soft curls, tender eyes, innocent,
lips caressing,
leaves me trembling.

Fear grips my tongue
as I try to speak,
the words might not
come out right.
Panic tightens the knot
in my throat as
impatience whips the silence.

His soft eyes beckon,
I attempt to move but
anxiety roots me in the spot.
I might fall into his arms,
tripped by weakness.
Yet my spirit
he embraces warmly.

His touch left traces
of his fragrance upon my breast,
I writhe in anticipation,
clinging desperately to the memories.
The crescendo will not last forever.
Soar now, with the melody
and unite with the chord
that makes for good music.

In Sweet Anticipation

I smiled
and walked hastily
to taste the sip of wine
upon your lips.

When evening shadows draw
curtains across the room,
and darkness locks the land
in a warm embrace.

Then in our closeness
I gaze upon your face
and lose myself in you.

Morning After

The aftermath.

The realization.

How I extended myself.

I recoiled in horror
at your audacity.

How you played
the keys of my heart
without regard
for tune or balance.

An unfinished chord
left hanging
in the air.
Yet,
the greatest melody
left untouched
by perfidious hands.

Out of Place

Flowers and candy, unknown to me,
fine dining but a fantasy.

Birthday is simply a number
on the calendar, forgotten.

I held my hand
alone as I walk.

Sweet nothings in my ear
a pleasure hoped for.

Silly messages
a dream.

All I'd ask is a goodbye kiss
'cept you don't exist.

Of Feminine Mystique

You asked me my name, I said "Pardon me Sir,
but my breeding does not allow conversations on the
street."

You invited me to tea, I accept graciously,
transported me in your car and held the door for me.

You poured me my tea and offered delightful treats,
I ate sparingly because- well that was neat.

Our conversations took us abroad and then back
home,
we spoke of the priesthood, of politicians and then
some.

You brushed the crumbs from my lap and then
straightened my hat,
but "my dear Sir, why couldn't you have left things
at that?

The closeness gave you a chance to take me in your
arms,
out the window flew my airs, at my feet fell the
charms.

At that moment, I was no longer a saint,
when our lips met and we kissed without restraint.

Dangerous Deception

Inside the fence
the flowering foliage beckons.
Shapely apples
tempt the passing honeybees,
while golden leaves
flirt with the afternoon sun.

But he could not resist
the shady bowers
so enticing,
and ventured in
to caress slender tree trunks
that flaunt their nakedness.

He only meant to stay
a little while,
but soon became intoxicated
with the sensuous wine
of nature's
grandest harvest.

Soon the golden sun
kissed her mistress goodbye,
and the fingers of
darkness crept silently
over the garden gate.

Unannounced
the master returned to find
muddy tracks
upon his gate,
his treasure stolen.

Had he waited a while,
reason would have courted him.
But he surrendered
to his vilest passion
and anger's foul breath
rose to claim its prize.

When the golden sun rose
to greet its mistress,
beneath the
morning dew
two corpses lay.

The Tattle Tale

Meticulously,
covertly weaving,
every stitch in place,
no time for other business,
no time for tatting lace.
Chain stitches here,
each tale connects
though the colors are different.

Blanket stitches there,
secure them in place
with a double knot here.
And at times
a stitch will start out neat
but very soon
in a slip stitch it is complete.

Stitching endlessly
the task is never done,
always some new tale to tell,
for her that is fun.

Unequivocally

And what should I say?
When your sugared words
become like brine upon my lips.
When the cobwebs from
your spidery designs
strangles the sincerity
of my heart.

And where should I go?
When my feet refuse to tread
in your misplaced footprints.
When the wind from
your insincere throat
puts locks
upon my doors.

And what should I do?
When your desperate vows
seek my shadow
across the empty room.
When you are left
standing still,
alone, regretting
the passing of time.

Tools of Trade

Oppression
they say
is what keeps you down,
but I say
the oppressed is
the one with a frown.

"It breaks your back"
they say,
"It's a terrible sin,"
but any oppressed
is he who
doesn't want to win.

For wars are fought
and only the
strongest survive,
and those who
pursue their goals
will win the prize.

In this life
many things we do lack,
but if you ask me I'll say,
"it's the brother who borrows
and doesn't repay,
he's the one
that's keeping you back."

The Truth Is

I didn't mean
to take off my shoe
so you could step
on my Achilles heel.
And then
I wouldn't have
minded it so,
only the pain
of deception
was real.

Ten years
have passed,
the deceit
still rings true,
in your voice,
your stories so blue.
A heart of stone
needs much turning,
Heaven's near
but Hell's
still burning.

Tricks of the Trade

When words
oozed out of
honeyed throats
to greet
their gilded smile.
And talk
worth more than
a penny,
not cheap,
of what to do
upon winning.

And the candidacy
becomes we,
not me,
as taxes are
struck off the book.
And many the saying
will do, will do,
but if it's done
that's good luck.

Of Myth and Dreams

Silently, stealthily,
you entered
my unwelcome dream.

And though my
charcoaled memory
seared your clayed feet,
yet you stayed
to relive a nightmare.

And when
your ghost like figure
danced about my brain,
it was to a tune that
had only a refrain.

So you kept going
back and forth
and to and fro,
causing much puzzlement
and furrowing my brow.

And when it was over
I still could not understand,
you left
without saying goodbye,
just an unwritten note
in my hand.

Solomon's Eyes

'Tis a wondrous thing
to be wise,
for wisdom has many eyes.

To see the things
the ordinary cannot see,
I dare say makes one
very extraordinary.

To possess good judgment
is a desirable trait,
since 'twixt good and bad
lies our fate.

Making Lemonade

It was not my choice,
'twas thrust upon me,
in an uncanny way
when I offered my hand.

An odd lemon,
dripping upon my floor
in many places. And
the acidity turns
my golden walk gray
causing me to slip,
scattering my trinkets
and creating despair.

Yet over the horizon
my cloud of despair reflects
a ray of light. And while
from my left hand
I lick the sour juice,
I add a lump of sugar
with my right,
and stir my glass
with a silver spoon.

Beyond the Aerie

Drawn back,
the stone in a catapult,
in the hands of a hunter,
pressed firmly
against his chest,
an arrow in the bow
of an archer,
in the line of his vision.
Humbly, painfully,
I waited
for the moment of release.

Yet but in a split second,
unaware of the timing
freedom came.
And then,
unfettered, and
boundless
I soared,
beyond
the hunter's aim,
beyond
the archer's range,
to the place
where the Eagles play.

Just a Bug Buggin'

There was a man
who came from very far.
He misplaced the truth
and thought that
made him foolproof.

But soon he felt very hot
and then he was cold,
was sure he had the fever
and wanted to see
the doctor.

He said he heard voices
but they came from within.
So he got up and
walked to and fro,
wiping sweat and
mopping his brow.

He had no idea of
what was happening,
it wasn't a sickness,
just his conscience
talking to him.

Detached

Broken promises,
broken dreams,
conceived in confusion,
bred in hate.
Driven by illusion,
steered by despair,
empowered
with one thought,
to create a Euphoria,
anywhere.

A new name,
A new place,
A new identity.
Longing to break free,
but still holding on
to the security
of being cocooned
in a cold stone
called home.

Of Truth and Lies

There is no truth
in a white lie,
you won't find it
if you try.

No harm
in black magic,
only a magician
can do tricks.

No coward
in a yellow belly,
there's some fear
in all of us already.

No blood
on a red neck,
you won't see it
if you check.

No need for strife
between you and me,
we're all made alike,
when we die you'll see.

A Healthy Habit

It is contagious
they say,
it is in the air,
it can get to
your head
if you're somewhere
out there.

You don't have to touch
they say,
you don't have
to inhale,
'cause when you smile
my friend
they'll smile
with you again.

Racing Demon

A jaywalker
they'd call me
had I been
in your path.
Countless lives
you have stolen
though you never stop,
just keep rolling.

And your hard heart
is cold though hot,
the scraps of
an imagination.
An incomplete
imitation
of God's holy
creation.

A Woman, A Tree, Me

Yesterday
I was the Poplar-
young and growing,
my body soft and tender-
my breasts were showing.

Evergreen as the Fir-
slender as the Birch,
and a Maple too-
on my branches
birds would perch.

For Christmas I was the spruce-
wearing lights and ornaments,
and other decorations if I choose-
surrounded by children,
ladies and gents.

Then I was the Elm-
and able to command a price,
for my body was
very valuable-
to those who thought it nice.

Fruit I had begun to bear-
Fig was then my name,
beautiful as the
Cypress or Cedar-
I was evergreen just the same.

Then I was the Aspen-
my leaves fluttered
in the lightest wind,

because I was old
and afflicted-
with the trembling.

Today I am a willow
and still good as a shade tree,
but now
I've taken to weeping-
my husband has passed on
and I'm left sorrowing.

A Penny for the Knowin'

I don't know
if I was wrong
to say what I said,
but all I know
if I should hold it
in any longer
I'd surely be dead.

It wasn't a joke you see,
it wasn't meant to be.
But when I say
I pay my own rent and
buy my own food,
that makes
me feel
quite liberated.

The Market Place

Themselves
they do scare-
Hyenas in the night,
snuffing and puffing-
a nasal drawl-indecent-
in consequence.

And the followers
of Bacchus
themselves beguile-
a mirrored image reflect-
thinking that evening
is morning
when morning is night.

.

Communicating with
Lady Liberty

She stands tall,
a torch in her hand.
Said her name is Liberty,
she is a symbol for the freed.
Then I asked her
on which few
it was conferred?

I took time out and explained
that being free
doesn't mean unchained,
but the liberty
to be who you are,
without having to state it
through war.

That the greatest freedom
is within
and to be prejudiced is sin,
for if I'm educated
and my money
can't get me anywhere
then indeed
I have a lot to fear.

My chain is heavier then
than the few behind bars,
for in time they'll be released
but mine I'll carry
until I'm deceased.

www.worry.com

It's this damn thing
they call the computer,
lately it has caused me
to feel like a loser.

My friend said she went surfing
but I could not understand
how can she surf
when the thing is on land.

Said she got on the Internet
and talked to a man in Japan,
but she didn't use the phone
she just typed letters with her hand.

Said she can do 'most anything
when she's 'on line',
from shopping at Macy's
to banking at the Dime.

Now this little thing
is causing me to fret,
when will I catch up,
I haven't started learning yet.

Love Incandescent

To me-
you are morn,
wiping the sleepy eyes
of dawn-
turning in a warm bed.

As yet-
a virginal forest
beckoning the eager hunter,
the snare-
a sensual dream.

And-
your deeds undone are
a tincture of memories,
the reality-
yet unknown.

A String of Pearls

Observe the beautiful pearl
and understand
how 'twas made,
when an irritant
such as a grain of sand
in the oyster's stomach
was laid.

'Tween the irritant
and itself,
a glossy mass
the oyster wears.
And after many days,
even weeks and
months and years
of covering with
this shiny mask
a fine pearl becomes
the object at last.

Observe beautiful lives
and understand
how they are made,
ofttimes before them
great obstacles are laid
yet on a chosen
path they stayed.

Turning misfortunes
into golden opportunities
with love, kindness

and deeds so divine,
'til they should become
like the treasure
of a string of pearls.

ABOUT THE AUTHOR

JACQUE DALEY received the *Editor's Choice Award* from *The National Library of Poetry* for outstanding achievement in Poetry for her contest entry *Of Man and Nature* published in *The Scenic Route*. She also has poetic contribution in their previous anthology *The Rippling Waters*. Other works include another poetry collection *Verses for Kids*, and an unpublished novel *Lead us not into Temptation*. She also writes for the *Urban Dialogue Magazine*.